Business with Purpose
Operating Business with Ethical Decisions
Biblical Principles

Authored by
Diana Gadus, M.Ed.

Business with Purpose
Operating Business with Ethical Decisions
Biblical Principles
Copyright 2024 by Diana Gadus, M.Ed.
Published by: Diana Gadus Inc.

Diana Gadus, Inc
8711 Wesleyan Dr
Fort Myers, Fl 33919

Preface

My name is Diana Gadus and I grew up in a family business which at peak performance, employed nearly sixty people. My parents immigrated to this country from Northern Jugoslavia from a little town that bordered Szeged Hungary back in the early 1960's. I am 100% Hungarian. My father was a tailor and he and my mother worked very hard. It was through their work ethic and what my father would call luck, that I learned that God exists. My father bought a third into a sewing factory that manufactured better women's sportswear. These clothes were nice business attire sold at locations such as Dillard's, Lampsons and Macy's in the women's business clothing section. Through my childhood experiences and my own journey into business practices, I learned many biblical principles and applications that are a strong foundation to business success. I am extremely blessed and highly favored to have the opportunity to share the ethical decisions in biblical principles used to operate good business practices that produce success and longevity.

Introduction

In a world increasingly driven by profit margins and competitive advantage, the concept of integrating faith with business practices might seem countercultural. Yet, for those who choose to operate their businesses grounded in biblical principles, the rewards extend far beyond financial success. "Business with Purpose: Operating Your Business with Ethical Decisions Based on Biblical Principles" is a comprehensive guide that explores how faith can serve as a guiding light in the often murky waters of commerce.

The United States, a sovereign nation founded on the tenet of religious freedom, embraces the mantra "One Nation Under God." This foundation provides a unique landscape where faith and enterprise can coexist harmoniously. My name is Diana Gadus, a seasoned real estate professional with over two decades of experience in education and a deep commitment to integrity and service. Through my journey, I have discovered that embedding biblical principles in every aspect of business operations not only fosters a healthy work environment but also creates a ripple effect of positive change in the community.

The biblical foundation for ethical business practices is laid out in scriptures such as Colossians 3:23-24 (NIV): "Whatever you do, work at it with all your heart, as working for the Lord, not for human masters, since you know that you will receive an inheritance from the Lord as a reward. It is the Lord Christ you are serving." This passage, among many others, underscores the importance of dedication, integrity, and service in our professional endeavors.

This book is structured to provide a comprehensive understanding of how to integrate these timeless principles into modern business practices. Each chapter delves into specific aspects of business management, from leadership and team building to financial stewardship and customer relations. Practical advice is intertwined with biblical teachings, providing a robust framework for making ethical decisions that honor God.

Throughout my career, I have earned the designations of Committed to Excellence, Senior Real Estate Specialist, and Resort and Second Home Property Specialist. These titles reflect my commitment to professionalism and excellence in service. However, my most significant achievement is the trust and respect of my clients and community, earned through unwavering integrity and dedication to their needs.

In "Business with Purpose," you will find actionable strategies, real-life examples, and scriptural insights designed to inspire and guide you. Whether you are a seasoned entrepreneur or just starting, this book offers valuable lessons on how to navigate the complexities of the business world while staying true to your faith. The journey of integrating biblical principles into your business is not without challenges, but the rewards—both spiritual and practical—are profound.

As you embark on this journey, remember the words of Proverbs 16:3 (NIV): "Commit to the Lord whatever you do, and he will establish your plans." May this book serve as a beacon, guiding you towards a business that not only thrives but also honors the greater purpose for which it was created.

Chapter 1

Foundations of Faith-Based Business Practices

The foundation of any successful venture is its core values and guiding principles. For a business operating with biblical principles at its heart, this foundation is built upon faith, integrity, and a commitment to serving God's purpose. The Bible provides a wealth of wisdom on how to conduct ourselves in our personal and professional lives, offering a blueprint for ethical business practices that stand the test of time.

In Matthew 7:24-25 (NIV), Jesus speaks of the wise man who built his house on the rock: "Therefore everyone who hears these words of mine and puts them into practice is like a wise man who built his house on the rock. The rain came down, the streams rose, and the winds blew and beat against that house; yet it did not fall, because it had its foundation on the rock." This parable emphasizes the importance of building our endeavors on a solid foundation—one that can withstand challenges and remain steadfast.

A faith-based business begins with the acknowledgment that God is the ultimate authority and provider. Recognizing this shifts our perspective from self-reliance to reliance on divine guidance. Proverbs 3:5-6 (NIV) reminds us, "Trust in the Lord with all your heart and lean not on your own understanding; in all your ways submit to him, and he will make your paths straight." By placing our trust in God and seeking His direction, we set the stage for a business that aligns with His will.

One of the first steps in establishing a faith-based business is defining its mission and vision in alignment with biblical values. This involves reflecting on scriptures that resonate with your purpose and integrating them into your business's core statements. For example, a mission statement might include a commitment to serving others with love and integrity, inspired by Mark 12:31 (NIV): "Love your neighbor as yourself."

Furthermore, it's essential to cultivate a culture that embodies these values. This means leading by example and fostering an environment where employees feel valued, respected, and encouraged to live out their faith. Ephesians 6:7 (NIV) advises, "Serve wholeheartedly, as if you were serving the Lord, not people." When leaders demonstrate genuine care and a servant-hearted attitude, it sets the tone for the entire organization.

Incorporating prayer and scripture into the daily operations of the business can also fortify its foundation. Regular prayer meetings, Bible studies, and devotional times can help keep the team focused on God's word and His guidance. Philippians 4:6 (NIV) encourages us, "Do not be anxious about anything, but in every situation, by prayer and petition, with thanksgiving, present your requests to God." By making prayer a cornerstone of your business, you invite God's presence and wisdom into every decision.

Building a faith-based business also involves being prepared for spiritual warfare and challenges. Ephesians 6:12 (NIV) states, "For our struggle is not against flesh and blood, but against the rulers, against the authorities, against the powers of this dark world and against the spiritual forces of evil in the heavenly realms." Understanding that obstacles may arise and being equipped with the armor of God (Ephesians 6:13-17) ensures that you can stand firm in your faith and principles.

Lastly, accountability is crucial in maintaining a faith-based business. Surrounding yourself with a community of believers who can provide support, encouragement, and constructive feedback helps to stay true to your values. Proverbs 27:17 (NIV) says, "As iron sharpens iron, so one person sharpens another." Having mentors, advisors, and peers who share your commitment to biblical principles can provide invaluable guidance and accountability.

In conclusion, the foundation of a faith-based business is rooted in unwavering trust in God, a commitment to biblical values, and a dedication to serving others. By building your business on these principles, you create a legacy that honors God and impacts your community positively. As you embark on this journey, remember to seek His guidance in all things, trusting that He will establish your plans and bless your efforts.

Chapter 2

Integrity in Every Transaction

Integrity is the cornerstone of any reputable business. It is the quality of being honest and having strong moral principles. In a faith-based business, integrity goes beyond mere compliance with laws and regulations; it is about aligning every action and decision with biblical teachings. Proverbs 10:9 (NIV) asserts, "Whoever walks in integrity walks securely, but whoever takes crooked paths will be found out." This verse highlights the security and stability that come from living and operating with integrity.

To integrate integrity into every transaction, it starts with personal commitment. As a business leader, your actions set the standard for your team. James 1:22 (NIV) advises, "Do not merely listen to the word, and so deceive yourselves. Do what it says." Living out your faith through integrity in business means being truthful in all communications, honoring commitments, and treating everyone with fairness and respect.

One practical way to uphold integrity is through transparency. Open and honest communication with clients, employees, and stakeholders fosters trust and credibility. In real estate, for example, this means providing accurate information about properties, being clear about terms and conditions, and not exaggerating benefits or hiding potential drawbacks. Luke 16:10 (NIV) teaches, "Whoever can be trusted with very little can also be trusted with much, and whoever is dishonest with very little will also be dishonest with much." Small acts of honesty build a foundation of trust that can handle larger responsibilities.

Additionally, ensuring that your business practices are fair and just is a critical aspect of integrity. This includes fair pricing, honoring warranties and guarantees, and being transparent about fees and charges. Leviticus 19:36 (NIV) instructs, "Use honest scales and honest weights, an honest ephah and an honest hin. I am the Lord your God, who brought you out of Egypt." By maintaining fair practices, you reflect God's justice and righteousness in your business operations.

Ethical decision-making is another key component of integrity. When faced with difficult choices, turning to scripture for guidance can help ensure that your decisions are aligned with biblical principles. Psalm 119:105 (NIV) says, "Your word is a lamp for my feet, a light on my path." By seeking wisdom from the Bible, you can navigate complex situations with integrity and confidence.

It's also important to foster a culture of accountability within your organization. This means creating an environment where employees feel comfortable speaking up about unethical behavior and where there are clear consequences for actions that compromise integrity. Galatians 6:1 (NIV) encourages, "Brothers and sisters, if someone is caught in a sin, you who live by the Spirit should restore that person gently. But watch yourselves, or you also may be tempted." Addressing issues with grace and firmness helps maintain a high standard of integrity.

Integrity in transactions also extends to how you handle finances. Proverbs 13:11 (NIV) warns, "Dishonest money dwindles away, but whoever gathers money little by little makes it grow." Ensuring that your financial practices are honest, transparent, and compliant with legal standards not only protects your business but also honors God. This includes accurate bookkeeping, fair compensation for employees, and responsible management of business resources.

Moreover, building strong relationships based on trust and integrity can lead to long-term success. Colossians 3:23-24 (NIV) reminds us, "Whatever you do, work at it with all your heart, as working for the Lord, not for human masters, since you know that you will receive an inheritance from the Lord as a reward. It is the Lord Christ you are serving." By serving clients, employees, and partners with integrity, you build a reputation that attracts loyalty and respect.

In conclusion, integrity is not just a business strategy; it is a reflection of your faith and commitment to living out biblical principles. By embedding integrity into every transaction, you create a trustworthy and respected business that honors God and serves the community. As you continue to operate with honesty and fairness, remember the words of Proverbs 21:3 (NIV): "To do what is right and just is more acceptable to the Lord than sacrifice." Let integrity be the guiding light in all your business endeavors.

Chapter 3

Stewardship: Managing Resources Wisely

Stewardship is a fundamental biblical principle that emphasizes the responsible management of resources. In a business context, stewardship involves effectively managing time, talent, and treasure to honor God and advance His purposes. The Bible offers numerous insights on how to be good stewards of the resources entrusted to us. Luke 12:42 (NIV) states, "The Lord answered, 'Who then is the faithful and wise manager, whom the master puts in charge of his servants to give them their food allowance at the proper time?'" This verse underscores the importance of wisdom and faithfulness in stewardship.

One of the first steps in practicing stewardship is recognizing that all resources ultimately belong to God. Psalm 24:1 (NIV) declares, "The earth is the Lord's, and everything in it, the world, and all who live in it." Acknowledging God's ownership helps shift our perspective from ownership to management. As stewards, we are responsible for using resources in ways that align with God's will.

Time is one of the most valuable resources we have. Ephesians 5:15-16 (NIV) advises, "Be very careful, then, how you live—not as unwise but as wise, making the most of every opportunity, because the days are evil." Effective time management involves setting priorities, planning ahead, and avoiding procrastination. In a business setting, this means creating efficient workflows, delegating tasks appropriately, and ensuring that time is spent on activities that add value to the organization.

Talent, or human resources, is another critical aspect of stewardship. 1 Peter 4:10 (NIV) encourages, "Each of you should use whatever gift you have received to serve others, as faithful stewards of God's grace in its various forms." Recognizing and nurturing the talents of employees not only benefits the business but also honors God by enabling individuals to fulfill their potential. This involves providing opportunities for professional development, encouraging creativity, and fostering a supportive work environment.

Financial stewardship is equally important. Proverbs 3:9-10 (NIV) instructs, "Honor the Lord with your wealth, with the firstfruits of all your crops; then your barns will be filled to overflowing, and your vats will brim over with new wine." Managing financial resources wisely involves budgeting, investing prudently, and being generous. A faith-based business should prioritize ethical financial practices, such as fair pricing, transparent accounting, and giving back to the community through charitable contributions.

Environmental stewardship is another dimension that aligns with biblical principles. Genesis 2:15 (NIV) states, "The Lord God took the man and put him in the Garden of Eden to work it and take care of it." Businesses have a responsibility to minimize their environmental impact by adopting sustainable practices. This can include reducing waste, conserving energy, and supporting eco-friendly initiatives. By caring for the environment, we honor God's creation and contribute to the well-being of future generations.

One practical approach to stewardship is implementing systems and processes that enhance efficiency and accountability. This can involve using technology to streamline operations, regularly reviewing performance metrics, and setting clear goals and objectives. Proverbs 21:5 (NIV) reminds us, "The plans of the diligent lead to profit as surely as haste leads to poverty." Thoughtful planning and diligent execution are essential components of effective stewardship.

Moreover, fostering a culture of stewardship within the organization encourages everyone to take responsibility for their actions and contributions. Colossians 3:23-24 (NIV) says, "Whatever you do, work at it with all your heart, as working for the Lord, not for human masters." When employees understand that their work is ultimately for God's glory, they are more likely to approach their tasks with diligence and care.

In conclusion, stewardship is a multifaceted principle that involves managing time, talent, and treasure in ways that honor God and advance His purposes. By practicing good stewardship, businesses can operate efficiently, ethically, and sustainably. As stewards, we are called to be faithful, wise, and diligent in managing the resources entrusted to us. As you integrate these principles into your business, remember the words of Matthew 25:21 (NIV): "His master replied, 'Well done, good and faithful servant! You have been faithful with a few things; I will put you in charge of many things. Come and share your master's happiness!'" Let stewardship be a guiding principle in all your endeavors, reflecting your commitment to God and His kingdom.

Chapter 4

23

Servant Leadership in the Workplace

Servant leadership is a transformative approach to leadership that emphasizes serving others first. This concept is deeply rooted in biblical teachings and stands in stark contrast to traditional models of leadership that prioritize authority and control. Jesus Christ himself exemplified servant leadership, as illustrated in Mark 10:45 (NIV): "For even the Son of Man did not come to be served, but to serve, and to give his life as a ransom for many." This chapter explores how to embody servant leadership in the workplace, creating an environment where employees feel valued, supported, and inspired.

At the heart of servant leadership is the principle of putting others' needs before your own. Philippians 2:3-4 (NIV) instructs, "Do nothing out of selfish ambition or vain conceit. Rather, in humility value others above yourselves, not looking to your own interests but each of you to the interests of the others." In a business context, this means prioritizing the well-being and development of employees, clients, and stakeholders. By doing so, leaders can foster a culture of mutual respect and collaboration.

One practical way to practice servant leadership is by actively listening to your team. James 1:19 (NIV) advises, "My dear brothers and sisters, take note of this: Everyone should be quick to listen, slow to speak and slow to become angry." Listening to employees' ideas, concerns, and feedback not only shows that you value their input but also provides valuable insights that can enhance the organization. Regular one-on-one meetings, open-door policies, and anonymous feedback channels can facilitate effective communication.

Empowering employees is another key aspect of servant leadership. This involves providing them with the resources, training, and autonomy they need to excel in their roles. Ephesians 4:11-12 (NIV) explains, "So Christ himself gave the apostles, the prophets, the evangelists, the pastors and teachers, to equip his people for works of service, so that the body of Christ may be built up." By equipping employees with the necessary tools and support, leaders enable them to perform at their best and contribute to the organization's success.

Servant leadership also requires a commitment to personal growth and development. As a leader, continually seeking to improve your skills and character sets an example for others to follow. Proverbs 27:17 (NIV) states, "As iron sharpens iron, so one person sharpens another." Engaging in ongoing learning, seeking mentorship, and being open to constructive criticism can help leaders grow and inspire their teams to do the same.

Creating a supportive and inclusive work environment is essential for servant leadership. Galatians 6:2 (NIV) encourages, "Carry each other's burdens, and in this way, you will fulfill the law of Christ." Leaders can foster a sense of community by promoting teamwork, recognizing and celebrating achievements, and providing support during challenging times. This not only enhances employee satisfaction and retention but also strengthens the overall cohesion of the organization.

Another important aspect of servant leadership is ethical behavior. Leaders must model integrity, honesty, and fairness in all their actions. Proverbs 11:3 (NIV) reminds us, "The integrity of the upright guides them, but the unfaithful are destroyed by their duplicity." By consistently demonstrating ethical behavior, leaders build trust and credibility, which are crucial for fostering a positive work environment and achieving long-term success.

Moreover, servant leadership involves a commitment to serving the community and making a positive impact beyond the business. Matthew 5:16 (NIV) encourages us, "In the same way, let your light shine before others, that they may see your good deeds and glorify your Father in heaven." By engaging in community service, supporting local initiatives, and promoting corporate social responsibility, businesses can extend their influence and embody the principles of servant leadership on a broader scale.

In conclusion, servant leadership is about leading with a heart of service, prioritizing the needs and growth of others, and fostering an environment of respect, support, and ethical behavior. By embodying these principles, leaders not only enhance their organizations but also reflect the teachings of Jesus Christ. As you strive to implement servant leadership in your workplace, remember the words of Matthew 20:26-28 (NIV): "Not so with you. Instead, whoever wants to become great among you must be your servant, and whoever wants to be first must be your slave—just as the Son of Man did not come to be served, but to serve, and to give his life as a ransom for many." Let this spirit of service guide your leadership journey, inspiring others and honoring God in all that you do.

Chapter 5

Building a Culture of Trust

Trust is the bedrock of any successful business relationship, whether it's between employer and employee, business and client, or company and community. A culture of trust fosters open communication, collaboration, and loyalty, all of which are essential for a thriving business. Proverbs 3:29 (NIV) advises, "Do not plot harm against your neighbor, who lives trustfully near you." This chapter delves into how to cultivate and maintain trust within your organization, ensuring that it becomes a foundational element of your business culture.

Creating a culture of trust begins with transparency. Open and honest communication about the company's goals, challenges, and decisions helps build credibility and trustworthiness. Ephesians 4:25 (NIV) emphasizes, "Therefore each of you must put off falsehood and speak truthfully to your neighbor, for we are all members of one body." Sharing information openly with your team and stakeholders fosters an environment where everyone feels informed, valued, and engaged.

Consistency is another critical component of building trust. James 1:17 (NIV) reminds us, "Every good and perfect gift is from above, coming down from the Father of the heavenly lights, who does not change like shifting shadows." Consistency in actions, values, and decision-making reassures employees and clients that the business operates on solid principles. This reliability forms the basis of trust and confidence in the organization.

Empathy plays a vital role in fostering trust. Philippians 2:4 (NIV) advises, "Not looking to your own interests but each of you to the interests of the others." Showing genuine concern for the well-being of employees and clients creates a bond of trust and mutual respect. This can be achieved through active listening, offering support during difficult times, and recognizing and appreciating contributions.

Accountability is essential in maintaining a culture of trust. Leaders must hold themselves and others accountable for their actions and decisions. Galatians 6:7 (NIV) states, "Do not be deceived: God cannot be mocked. A man reaps what he sows." When mistakes occur, acknowledging them, taking responsibility, and making amends demonstrates integrity and fosters trust. Establishing clear expectations and providing constructive feedback also contribute to a culture of accountability.

Empowering employees is another key aspect of building trust. When employees feel trusted to make decisions and take ownership of their work, they are more likely to be engaged and motivated. Proverbs 31:11 (NIV) speaks of a virtuous woman, "Her husband has full confidence in her and lacks nothing of value." By trusting employees with responsibilities and providing the necessary support, leaders can cultivate a sense of autonomy and trustworthiness.

Building trust with clients involves delivering on promises and exceeding expectations. Matthew 5:37 (NIV) instructs, "All you need to say is simply 'Yes' or 'No'; anything beyond this comes from the evil one." Honoring commitments and being transparent about what can and cannot be delivered ensures that clients feel valued and respected. Providing excellent customer service and addressing concerns promptly further solidifies trust.

Moreover, fostering a culture of trust involves creating a safe and inclusive environment where everyone feels respected and valued. Galatians 3:28 (NIV) reminds us, "There is neither Jew nor Gentile, neither slave nor free, nor is there male and female, for you are all one in Christ Jesus." Embracing diversity, promoting equality, and ensuring that all voices are heard and respected contribute to a trusting and collaborative workplace.

In conclusion, building a culture of trust requires transparency, consistency, empathy, accountability, empowerment, and inclusivity. By prioritizing these elements, leaders can create a trusting environment that fosters collaboration, loyalty, and long-term success. As you work to build and maintain trust within your organization, remember the words of Proverbs 16:20 (NIV): "Whoever gives heed to instruction prospers, and blessed is the one who trusts in the Lord." Let trust be the cornerstone of your business culture, guiding your interactions and decisions, and honoring God in all that you do.

Chapter 6

Ethical Decision-Making Frameworks

In the complex world of business, ethical decision-making is crucial. It involves choosing actions that are right, fair, and just, aligning with both legal standards and moral principles. For a faith-based business, ethical decision-making is guided by biblical principles. Proverbs 2:9 (NIV) says, "Then you will understand what is right and just and fair—every good path." This chapter explores frameworks for making ethical decisions that honor God and uphold integrity in business practices.

The first step in ethical decision-making is identifying the ethical issue at hand. This requires sensitivity to recognize situations where moral principles may be at stake. James 4:17 (NIV) states, "If anyone, then, knows the good they ought to do and doesn't do it, it is sin for them." Being aware of potential ethical dilemmas is the foundation for addressing them appropriately.

Next, it's important to gather all relevant information. Proverbs 18:13 (NIV) advises, "To answer before listening—that is folly and shame." Understanding the facts, the stakeholders involved, and the possible consequences of various actions ensures a well-informed decision. This thorough approach prevents hasty judgments and promotes fairness.

Consulting the Bible and seeking God's guidance through prayer are essential steps in the decision-making process. Psalm 119:105 (NIV) declares, "Your word is a lamp for my feet, a light on my path." By reflecting on scripture and praying for wisdom, business leaders can align their decisions with God's will. Verses such as Micah 6:8 (NIV) offer clear ethical directives: "He has shown you, O mortal, what is good. And what does the Lord require of you? To act justly and to love mercy and to walk humbly with your God."

Considering the impact of decisions on all stakeholders is another key component. Philippians 2:3-4 (NIV) encourages, "Do nothing out of selfish ambition or vain conceit. Rather, in humility value others above yourselves, not looking to your own interests but each of you to the interests of the others." Ethical decisions should take into account the well-being of employees, clients, suppliers, and the community. This holistic approach ensures that actions are just and beneficial to all involved.

Moreover, seeking counsel from trusted advisors can provide valuable perspectives and insights. Proverbs 15:22 (NIV) states, "Plans fail for lack of counsel, but with many advisers they succeed." Engaging with mentors, colleagues, or a board of directors can help identify potential pitfalls and refine the decision-making process. These advisors can offer wisdom and experience that enrich the ethical considerations of a decision.

Implementing the decision with transparency and integrity is crucial. Matthew 5:37 (NIV) instructs, "All you need to say is simply 'Yes' or 'No'; anything beyond this comes from the evil one." Clear communication about the decision, the reasoning behind it, and its implications fosters trust and respect. This openness ensures that stakeholders understand the ethical considerations involved and can support the decision.

Finally, reflecting on the outcome and learning from the experience is an essential part of ethical decision-making. Proverbs 4:7 (NIV) emphasizes, "The beginning of wisdom is this: Get wisdom. Though it cost all you have, get understanding." Evaluating the results of a decision and its impact helps refine future decision-making processes and reinforces a commitment to ethical practices.

In conclusion, ethical decision-making in business involves identifying ethical issues, gathering information, consulting scripture, considering the impact on stakeholders, seeking counsel, implementing decisions with transparency, and reflecting on the outcomes. By following these steps and grounding decisions in biblical principles, business leaders can navigate complex situations with integrity and honor God in their actions. As you strive to make ethical decisions, remember the wisdom of Proverbs 3:5-6 (NIV): "Trust in the Lord with all your heart and lean not on your own understanding; in all your ways submit to him, and he will make your paths straight." Let these principles guide your ethical decision-making, ensuring that your business reflects your faith and values.

Chapter 7

Balancing Profit and Purpose

Balancing profit and purpose is a critical challenge for faith-based businesses. While financial success is necessary for sustainability, a higher purpose rooted in biblical principles should guide the overall mission. Matthew 6:33 (NIV) encourages, "But seek first his kingdom and his righteousness, and all these things will be given to you as well." This chapter explores how to achieve a harmonious balance between profitability and fulfilling a God-given purpose.

The first step in balancing profit and purpose is defining the core mission of the business. This mission should reflect both financial goals and a commitment to serving God's purpose. Colossians 3:23-24 (NIV) reminds us, "Whatever you do, work at it with all your heart, as working for the Lord, not for human masters, since you know that you will receive an inheritance from the Lord as a reward." By clearly articulating the business's mission, leaders can ensure that all activities align with both profit and purpose.

Integrating purpose into business operations involves setting goals that reflect both financial and spiritual objectives. Proverbs 16:3 (NIV) advises, "Commit to the Lord whatever you do, and he will establish your plans." This means establishing measurable targets for revenue and profitability, while also setting goals for community service, ethical practices, and spiritual growth. By tracking progress in both areas, businesses can maintain a balance between financial success and purposeful impact.

Corporate social responsibility (CSR) is an effective way to blend profit and purpose. This involves adopting practices that benefit society and the environment, beyond the immediate financial interests of the business. James 2:14-17 (NIV) emphasizes the importance of actions reflecting faith: "What good is it, my brothers and sisters, if someone claims to have faith but has no deeds? Can such faith save them? ... Faith by itself, if it is not accompanied by action, is dead." By engaging in CSR initiatives, businesses demonstrate their commitment to a higher purpose while enhancing their reputation and relationships with stakeholders.

Ethical sourcing and fair trade practices are other avenues to balance profit and purpose. Ensuring that products are sourced ethically and workers are treated fairly reflects the biblical principle of justice. Isaiah 1:17 (NIV) urges, "Learn to do right; seek justice. Defend the oppressed. Take up the cause of the fatherless; plead the case of the widow." By prioritizing ethical practices, businesses can contribute to social equity while still achieving profitability.

Moreover, fostering a purpose-driven culture within the organization ensures that employees are aligned with the business's mission. This involves regular communication about the business's goals, values, and purpose, as well as encouraging employee involvement in community service and ethical initiatives. 1 Peter 4:10 (NIV) advises, "Each of you should use whatever gift you have received to serve others, as faithful stewards of God's grace in its various forms." By empowering employees to contribute to the business's purpose, leaders can create a motivated and cohesive team.

Marketing with a mission is another strategy to balance profit and purpose. By highlighting the business's commitment to ethical practices, community service, and spiritual values in marketing efforts, businesses can attract customers who share these values. Matthew 5:16 (NIV) encourages, "In the same way, let your light shine before others, that they may see your good deeds and glorify your Father in heaven." Purpose-driven marketing not only differentiates the business but also reinforces its commitment to serving God's purpose.

In conclusion, balancing profit and purpose involves defining a mission that encompasses both financial goals and spiritual values, setting measurable objectives, engaging in corporate social responsibility, practicing ethical sourcing, fostering a purpose-driven culture, and marketing with a mission. By integrating these strategies, businesses can achieve financial success while fulfilling a higher purpose. As you strive to balance profit and purpose, remember the wisdom of Proverbs 22:1 (NIV): "A good name is more desirable than great riches; to be esteemed is better than silver or gold." Let this principle guide your efforts, ensuring that your business reflects your faith and serves God's kingdom.

Chapter 8

40

Nurturing a Faith-Driven Team

A faith-driven team is essential for a business that seeks to operate on biblical principles. Building and nurturing such a team involves creating an environment where faith is encouraged, values are shared, and spiritual growth is supported. Ecclesiastes 4:9-10 (NIV) states, "Two are better than one, because they have a good return for their labor: If either of them falls down, one can help the other up." This chapter explores how to cultivate a team that is united in faith and purpose, driving the business towards its God-given mission.

The foundation of a faith-driven team is hiring individuals who share the business's values and commitment to biblical principles. Proverbs 27:17 (NIV) says, "As iron sharpens iron, so one person sharpens another." During the hiring process, it's important to look for candidates who not only possess the necessary skills and experience but also demonstrate a commitment to integrity, service, and faith. Conducting interviews that explore a candidate's values, ethical perspectives, and faith journey can help identify individuals who will thrive in a faith-driven environment.

Creating a supportive and inclusive workplace culture is crucial for nurturing a faith-driven team. This involves fostering an environment where employees feel valued, respected, and encouraged to express their faith. Colossians 3:12-14 (NIV) advises, "Therefore, as God's chosen people, holy and dearly loved, clothe yourselves with compassion, kindness, humility, gentleness and patience. Bear with each other and forgive one another ... And over all these virtues put on love, which binds them all together in perfect unity." By promoting these virtues, leaders can create a cohesive and supportive team.

Encouraging spiritual growth and development is another key aspect of nurturing a faith-driven team. This can be achieved through regular prayer meetings, Bible studies, and opportunities for fellowship. Hebrews 10:24-25 (NIV) encourages, "And let us consider how we may spur one another on toward love and good deeds, not giving up meeting together, as some are in the habit of doing, but encouraging one another." Providing time and space for employees to engage in spiritual practices fosters a sense of community and strengthens their faith.

Moreover, recognizing and celebrating employees' contributions and achievements is important for maintaining motivation and morale. 1 Thessalonians 5:11 (NIV) urges, "Therefore encourage one another and build each other up, just as in fact you are doing." Regularly acknowledging employees' hard work, both publicly and privately, shows appreciation and reinforces their value to the team. This recognition can be tied to both professional accomplishments and contributions to the business's faith-driven mission.

Providing opportunities for professional and personal growth is essential for nurturing a faith-driven team. Offering training programs, mentorship, and career development opportunities not only enhances employees' skills but also demonstrates a commitment to their overall well-being. Proverbs 22:29 (NIV) states, "Do you see someone skilled in their work? They will serve before kings; they will not serve before officials of low rank." By investing in employees' growth, leaders can cultivate a highly skilled and dedicated team.

Fostering open and transparent communication is critical for building trust and unity within the team. Ephesians 4:15 (NIV) encourages, "Instead, speaking the truth in love, we will grow to become in every respect the mature body of him who is the head, that is, Christ." Regular team meetings, open-door policies, and platforms for feedback ensure that employees feel heard and involved in the business's decisions and direction. This openness fosters a sense of belonging and commitment to the business's mission.

In conclusion, nurturing a faith-driven team involves hiring

individuals who share the business's values, creating a supportive workplace culture, encouraging spiritual growth, recognizing contributions, providing growth opportunities, and fostering open communication. By implementing these strategies, leaders can build a team that is united in faith and purpose, driving the business towards its God-given mission. As you work to cultivate a faith-driven team, remember the wisdom of Proverbs 27:17 (NIV): "As iron sharpens iron, so one person sharpens another." Let this principle guide your efforts, ensuring that your team reflects your faith and serves God's kingdom.

Chapter 9

45

Marketing with Morals

Marketing with morals involves promoting your business in a way that aligns with biblical principles and ethical standards. It's about being honest, transparent, and respectful in all marketing efforts, ensuring that the business's values are communicated effectively. Proverbs 11:1 (NIV) states, "The Lord detests dishonest scales, but accurate weights find favor with him." This chapter explores strategies for ethical marketing that build trust and honor God.

The foundation of moral marketing is honesty. This means providing accurate information about products or services, avoiding exaggeration, and ensuring that all claims are substantiated. Colossians 3:9 (NIV) instructs, "Do not lie to each other, since you have taken off your old self with its practices." By being truthful in advertising and promotions, businesses build credibility and trust with their audience.

Transparency is another key aspect of ethical marketing. Ephesians 4:25 (NIV) advises, "Therefore each of you must put off falsehood and speak truthfully to your neighbor, for we are all members of one body." This involves being open about pricing, terms and conditions, and potential risks or limitations of products or services. Clear and honest communication fosters trust and ensures that customers make informed decisions.

Respecting the audience is crucial in moral marketing. This means avoiding manipulative tactics, respecting privacy, and being sensitive to cultural and social values. Matthew 7:12 (NIV) encourages, "So in everything, do to others what you would have them do to you, for this sums up the Law and the Prophets." By treating customers with respect and dignity, businesses can create positive and lasting relationships.

Additionally, highlighting the business's commitment to ethical practices and community service can enhance its reputation and appeal. Matthew 5:16 (NIV) encourages, "In the same way, let your light shine before others, that they may see your good deeds and glorify your Father in heaven." Sharing stories of community involvement, charitable initiatives, and ethical sourcing practices in marketing materials can attract customers who value these principles.

Building a strong brand identity based on biblical values is another effective strategy. This involves consistently communicating the business's mission, vision, and values across all marketing channels. 1 Peter 2:12 (NIV) advises, "Live such good lives among the pagans that, though they accuse you of doing wrong, they may see your good deeds and glorify God on the day he visits us." A strong, values-based brand identity differentiates the business and resonates with like-minded customers.

Ethical marketing also includes being responsible with data and customer information. Proverbs 10:9 (NIV) reminds us, "Whoever walks in integrity walks securely, but whoever takes crooked paths will be found out." Ensuring data privacy and security, being transparent about data usage, and obtaining proper consent demonstrate respect for customers' rights and build trust.

Furthermore, providing excellent customer service is an integral part of ethical marketing. Philippians 2:3-4 (NIV) encourages, "Do nothing out of selfish ambition or vain conceit. Rather, in humility value others above yourselves, not looking to your own interests but each of you to the interests of the others." By prioritizing customer satisfaction, addressing concerns promptly, and treating customers with kindness and respect, businesses can enhance their reputation and foster loyalty.

In conclusion, marketing with morals involves honesty, transparency, respect, highlighting ethical practices, building a strong brand identity, responsible data management, and excellent customer service. By integrating these strategies, businesses can promote their products and services in a way that aligns with biblical principles and ethical standards. As you strive to market your business ethically, remember the wisdom of Proverbs 21:3 (NIV): "To do what is right and just is more acceptable to the Lord than sacrifice." Let this principle guide your marketing efforts, ensuring that your business reflects your faith and values.

A faith-driven team is essential for a business that seeks to operate on biblical principles. Building and nurturing such a team involves creating an environment where faith is encouraged, values are shared, and spiritual growth is supported. Ecclesiastes 4:9-10 (NIV) states, "Two are better than one, because they have a good return for their labor: If either of them falls down, one can help the other up." This chapter explores how to cultivate a team that is united in faith and purpose, driving the business towards its God-given mission.

The foundation of a faith-driven team is hiring individuals who share the business's values and commitment to biblical principles. Proverbs 27:17 (NIV) says, "As iron sharpens iron, so one person sharpens another." During the hiring process, it's important to look for candidates who not only possess the necessary skills and experience but also demonstrate a commitment to integrity, service, and faith. Conducting interviews that explore a candidate's values, ethical perspectives,

Chapter 10

51

Customer Relations: Love Thy Neighbor

In the realm of business, customer relations are paramount. Building and maintaining strong relationships with customers is essential for long-term success and reflects the biblical command to love our neighbors. Mark 12:31 (NIV) states, "The second is this: 'Love your neighbor as yourself.' There is no commandment greater than these." This chapter explores how to foster positive customer relations by treating customers with respect, kindness, and integrity.

The foundation of excellent customer relations is empathy. Philippians 2:4 (NIV) advises, "Not looking to your own interests but each of you to the interests of the others." Understanding and addressing the needs, concerns, and desires of customers create a strong bond of trust and loyalty. Active listening, personalized service, and showing genuine care for customers' well-being are key aspects of empathetic customer relations.

Integrity is another critical component of customer relations. Proverbs 12:22 (NIV) emphasizes, "The Lord detests lying lips, but he delights in people who are trustworthy." Being honest and transparent in all interactions, from marketing to post-purchase support, ensures that customers feel respected and valued. This includes providing accurate information, keeping promises, and addressing issues promptly and fairly.

Providing exceptional customer service is essential for fostering positive relationships. Colossians 3:23-24 (NIV) reminds us, "Whatever you do, work at it with all your heart, as working for the Lord, not for human masters." Going above and beyond to meet and exceed customer expectations demonstrates a commitment to excellence and service. This can involve prompt responses to inquiries, resolving issues efficiently, and consistently delivering high-quality products or services.

Building trust with customers involves being consistent and reliable. James 1:17 (NIV) states, "Every good and perfect gift is from above, coming down from the Father of the heavenly lights, who does not change like shifting shadows." Consistency in quality, service, and communication reassures customers that they can depend on the business. This reliability fosters long-term loyalty and positive word-of-mouth referrals.

Moreover, fostering a sense of community among customers can enhance relationships. Romans 12:10 (NIV) encourages, "Be devoted to one another in love. Honor one another above yourselves." Creating opportunities for customers to connect with each other and with the business, such as through events, social media engagement, or loyalty programs, builds a sense of belonging and mutual support.

Handling customer complaints with grace and humility is crucial for maintaining positive relations. Proverbs 15:1 (NIV) advises, "A gentle answer turns away wrath, but a harsh word stirs up anger." Addressing complaints promptly, listening to the customer's perspective, and offering fair solutions demonstrate respect and a commitment to customer satisfaction. Apologizing when mistakes are made and taking steps to prevent future issues show integrity and responsibility.

Recognizing and appreciating customers is another important aspect of building strong relationships. 1 Thessalonians 5:11 (NIV) urges, "Therefore encourage one another and build each other up, just as in fact you are doing." Showing gratitude through thank-you notes, special offers, or personalized messages reinforces customers' value and strengthens their connection to the business.

In conclusion, customer relations are built on empathy, integrity, exceptional service, consistency, community, grace, and appreciation. By treating customers with respect, kindness, and honesty, businesses can foster long-lasting relationships that reflect the biblical command to love our neighbors. As you work to enhance customer relations, remember the wisdom of Proverbs 3:3-4 (NIV): "Let love and faithfulness never leave you; bind them around your neck, write them on the tablet of your heart. Then you will win favor and a good name in the sight of God and man." Let this principle guide your interactions, ensuring that your business honors God and serves His people.

Chapter 11

Conflict Resolution with Grace

Conflict is an inevitable part of any business environment. How conflicts are handled can significantly impact relationships and the overall health of the organization. Resolving conflicts with grace, guided by biblical principles, can lead to stronger bonds and a more harmonious workplace. Matthew 5:9 (NIV) states, "Blessed are the peacemakers, for they will be called children of God." This chapter explores strategies for resolving conflicts gracefully, fostering a culture of peace and understanding.

The first step in conflict resolution is approaching the situation with a spirit of humility and understanding. Philippians 2:3 (NIV) advises, "Do nothing out of selfish ambition or vain conceit. Rather, in humility, value others above yourselves." Recognizing that everyone has unique perspectives and valid concerns sets the stage for constructive dialogue. Approaching conflicts with an open mind and a willingness to listen helps create an environment where resolution is possible.

Active listening is crucial for understanding the root causes of conflict. James 1:19 (NIV) encourages, "My dear brothers and sisters, take note of this: Everyone should be quick to listen, slow to speak and slow to become angry." Listening attentively to all parties involved ensures that their concerns are heard and acknowledged. This empathy can de-escalate tensions and foster a collaborative approach to finding solutions.

Seeking common ground is another key aspect of conflict resolution. Romans 12:18 (NIV) advises, "If it is possible, as far as it depends on you, live at peace with everyone." Identifying shared goals and interests helps shift the focus from the conflict itself to working together towards a mutually beneficial outcome. This collaborative mindset encourages cooperation and reduces adversarial attitudes.

Effective communication is essential for resolving conflicts. Ephesians 4:29 (NIV) states, "Do not let any unwholesome talk come out of your mouths, but only what is helpful for building others up according to their needs, that it may benefit those who listen." Clear, respectful, and constructive communication fosters understanding and helps clarify misunderstandings. Avoiding blame and focusing on solutions promotes a positive dialogue.

Forgiveness plays a vital role in resolving conflicts and restoring relationships. Colossians 3:13 (NIV) instructs, "Bear with each other and forgive one another if any of you has a grievance against someone. Forgive as the Lord forgave you."

Letting go of grudges and extending forgiveness helps heal wounds and move forward. This grace not only resolves the immediate conflict but also strengthens the overall relationship.

Establishing clear and fair conflict resolution policies can help manage disputes effectively. Proverbs 15:22 (NIV) says, "Plans fail for lack of counsel, but with many advisers they succeed." Having established procedures for addressing conflicts ensures that issues are handled consistently and fairly. This structure provides a roadmap for resolving disputes and reinforces the business's commitment to integrity and justice.

Involving a neutral third party or mediator can be beneficial in resolving more complex conflicts. Matthew 18:15-17 (NIV) outlines a process for addressing grievances within the community, including seeking the help of others if needed. A neutral mediator can facilitate communication, ensure that all perspectives are considered, and help find a fair resolution. This impartial guidance can be invaluable in achieving a just outcome.

In conclusion, resolving conflicts with grace involves humility, active listening, seeking common ground, effective communication, forgiveness, clear policies, and sometimes mediation. By handling conflicts in a manner that reflects biblical principles, businesses can foster a culture of peace, understanding, and mutual respect. As you navigate conflicts, remember the wisdom of Proverbs 19:11 (NIV): "A person's wisdom yields patience; it is to one's glory to overlook an offense." Let this principle guide your conflict resolution efforts, ensuring that your business honors God and maintains harmony.

Chapter 12

Financial Stewardship and Generosity

Financial stewardship and generosity are fundamental aspects of operating a faith-based business. Managing finances wisely and giving generously reflect biblical principles and contribute to the business's sustainability and positive impact. Proverbs 3:9-10 (NIV) instructs, "Honor the Lord with your wealth, with the firstfruits of all your crops; then your barns will be filled to overflowing, and your vats will brim over with new wine." This chapter explores strategies for effective financial stewardship and fostering a culture of generosity.

The foundation of financial stewardship is recognizing that all resources ultimately belong to God. Psalm 24:1 (NIV) declares, "The earth is the Lord's, and everything in it, the world, and all who live in it." Acknowledging God's ownership shifts our perspective from ownership to stewardship. This mindset encourages responsible and ethical management of financial resources, ensuring that they are used to honor God and advance His purposes.

Budgeting is a critical component of financial stewardship. Luke 14:28 (NIV) advises, "Suppose one of you wants to build a tower. Won't you first sit down and estimate the cost to see if you have enough money to complete it?" Creating and adhering to a budget helps businesses plan for expenses, manage cash flow, and allocate resources effectively. A well-structured budget ensures that the business operates within its means and can respond to financial challenges.

Prudent financial management also involves avoiding debt whenever possible. Proverbs 22:7 (NIV) warns, "The rich rule over the poor, and the borrower is slave to the lender." Minimizing debt reduces financial risk and enhances the business's stability. This can be achieved through careful planning, maintaining an emergency fund, and making strategic investments that promote long-term growth without compromising financial health.

Generosity is a vital expression of financial stewardship. Acts 20:35 (NIV) recounts, "In everything I did, I showed you that by this kind of hard work we must help the weak, remembering the words the Lord Jesus himself said: 'It is more blessed to give than to receive.'" Incorporating generosity into business operations involves supporting charitable causes, providing fair compensation to employees, and giving back to the community. This generosity not only reflects biblical values but also enhances the business's reputation and impact.

Tithing is a practice that exemplifies financial stewardship and generosity. Malachi 3:10 (NIV) encourages, "Bring the whole tithe into the storehouse, that there may be food in my house. Test me in this," says the Lord Almighty, "and see if I will not throw open the floodgates of heaven and pour out so much blessing that there will not be room enough to store it." Setting aside a portion of the business's income for charitable giving demonstrates trust in God's provision and commitment to supporting His work.

Transparent financial practices are essential for building trust and accountability. 2 Corinthians 8:21 (NIV) emphasizes, "For we are taking pains to do what is right, not only in the eyes of the Lord but also in the eyes of man." Ensuring that financial records are accurate, accessible, and regularly audited fosters transparency and integrity. This openness reassures stakeholders that the business is managed ethically and responsibly.

Furthermore, investing in the growth and development of employees is a form of generosity that benefits the business and its people. Proverbs 11:25 (NIV) states, "A generous person will prosper; whoever refreshes others will be refreshed." Providing opportunities for professional development, fair wages, and a supportive work environment demonstrates a commitment to employees' well-being and growth.

In conclusion, financial stewardship and generosity involve recognizing God's ownership of resources, budgeting wisely, minimizing debt, practicing generosity, tithing, maintaining transparent financial practices, and investing in employees. By integrating these principles, businesses can manage finances responsibly and make a positive impact on their communities. As you strive to be a good steward of your business's resources, remember the wisdom of 1 Timothy 6:18-19 (NIV): "Command them to do good, to be rich in good deeds, and to be generous and willing to share. In this way they will lay up treasure for themselves as a firm foundation for the coming age, so that they may take hold of the life that is truly life." Let this principle guide your financial stewardship and generosity, ensuring that your business honors God and serves His kingdom.

Chapter 13

Sustainable Business Practices

Sustainable business practices are essential for long-term success and stewardship of God's creation. Implementing environmentally responsible strategies reflects a commitment to preserving the earth and honoring God's mandate to care for it. Genesis 2:15 (NIV) states, "The Lord God took the man and put him in the Garden of Eden to work it and take care of it." This chapter explores how to integrate sustainable practices into business operations, ensuring that the business contributes positively to the environment.

The first step in adopting sustainable practices is conducting an environmental audit to assess the business's current impact. Proverbs 27:23 (NIV) advises, "Be sure you know the condition of your flocks, give careful attention to your herds." Understanding the business's energy consumption, waste production, and resource usage helps identify areas for improvement. This audit provides a baseline for setting sustainability goals and tracking progress.

Reducing waste is a fundamental aspect of sustainability. Proverbs 12:27 (NIV) states, "The lazy do not roast any game, but the diligent feed on the riches of the hunt." Implementing practices such as recycling, composting, and reducing single-use plastics can significantly minimize waste. Encouraging employees to adopt these practices and providing the necessary infrastructure, such as recycling bins and compost stations, ensures that waste reduction becomes a part of the business culture.

Energy efficiency is another key component of sustainable business practices. Psalm 24:1 (NIV) reminds us, "The earth is the Lord's, and everything in it." Investing in energy-efficient technologies, such as LED lighting, energy-efficient appliances, and renewable energy sources, reduces the business's carbon footprint. Conducting regular energy audits and seeking ways to optimize energy use can lead to significant savings and environmental benefits.

Sustainable sourcing involves choosing suppliers and materials that align with ethical and environmental standards. Proverbs 31:16 (NIV) highlights the importance of thoughtful procurement: "She considers a field and buys it; out of her earnings she plants a vineyard." Prioritizing suppliers who practice fair trade, use sustainable materials, and minimize environmental impact ensures that the business supports responsible practices throughout its supply chain.

Supporting local and sustainable businesses is another way to promote sustainability. By sourcing products and services locally, businesses can reduce their carbon footprint and support the local economy. Acts 20:35 (NIV) emphasizes the value of supporting others: "In everything I did, I showed you that by this kind of hard work we must help the weak." Partnering with local suppliers and promoting community-based initiatives fosters a network of sustainable practices.

Educating employees and stakeholders about sustainability is crucial for fostering a culture of environmental responsibility. Hosea 4:6 (NIV) warns, "My people are destroyed from lack of knowledge." Providing training on sustainable practices, sharing resources on environmental stewardship, and encouraging participation in sustainability initiatives ensure that everyone is aligned with the business's sustainability goals.

Measuring and reporting on sustainability efforts is essential for transparency and accountability. 2 Corinthians 8:21 (NIV) emphasizes the importance of doing what is right: "For we are taking pains to do what is right, not only in the eyes of the Lord but also in the eyes of man." Regularly publishing sustainability reports that detail the business's environmental impact, goals, and progress fosters transparency and encourages continuous improvement.

In conclusion, sustainable business practices involve conducting environmental audits, reducing waste, improving energy efficiency, sustainable sourcing, supporting local businesses, educating employees, and measuring and reporting efforts. By integrating these practices, businesses can honor God's mandate to care for the earth and contribute positively to the environment. As you strive to implement sustainable practices, remember the wisdom of Proverbs 16:3 (NIV): "Commit to the Lord whatever you do, and he will establish your plans." Let this principle guide your sustainability efforts, ensuring that your business honors God and preserves His creation for future generations.

Chapter 14

Navigating Challenges with Faith

Challenges are an inevitable part of running a business. Navigating these challenges with faith ensures that decisions and actions align with biblical principles and reflect trust in God's guidance. James 1:2-3 (NIV) encourages, "Consider it pure joy, my brothers and sisters, whenever you face trials of many kinds, because you know that the testing of your faith produces perseverance." This chapter explores strategies for facing business challenges with faith, resilience, and trust in God.

The first step in navigating challenges with faith is seeking God's guidance through prayer. Philippians 4:6 (NIV) advises, "Do not be anxious about anything, but in every situation, by prayer and petition, with thanksgiving, present your requests to God." Regular prayer and seeking God's wisdom provide clarity and peace in difficult times. Trusting that God is in control and has a plan for every situation helps reduce anxiety and fosters confidence.

Embracing a positive mindset is crucial for overcoming challenges. Romans 8:28 (NIV) reminds us, "And we know that in all things God works for the good of those who love him, who have been called according to his purpose." Viewing challenges as opportunities for growth and learning helps maintain a hopeful perspective. This optimism encourages resilience and fosters a proactive approach to problem-solving.

Relying on scripture for strength and guidance is essential during challenging times. Psalm 119:105 (NIV) declares, "Your word is a lamp for my feet, a light on my path." Turning to the Bible for inspiration and direction provides a solid foundation for decision-making. Verses such as Isaiah 41:10 (NIV) offer reassurance: "So do not fear, for I am with you; do not be dismayed, for I am your God. I will strengthen you and help you; I will uphold you with my righteous right hand."

Seeking support from a community of believers can provide encouragement and wisdom. Ecclesiastes 4:9-10 (NIV) states, "Two are better than one, because they have a good return for their labor: If either of them falls down, one can help the other up." Engaging with mentors, advisors, and peers who share your faith offers valuable insights and support. This community can provide prayer, counsel, and practical assistance during challenging times.

Developing resilience involves learning from past experiences and adapting to new circumstances. Romans 5:3-4 (NIV) teaches, "Not only so, but we also glory in our sufferings, because we know that suffering produces perseverance;

perseverance, character; and character, hope." Reflecting on previous challenges and identifying lessons learned helps build resilience and prepares the business for future obstacles. This adaptability is crucial for navigating a dynamic business environment.

Maintaining integrity and ethical standards, even in difficult times, is essential for honoring God and preserving trust. Proverbs 11:3 (NIV) reminds us, "The integrity of the upright guides them, but the unfaithful are destroyed by their duplicity." Upholding biblical principles and ethical practices, regardless of the circumstances, demonstrates faith and commitment. This integrity fosters trust and respect among employees, clients, and stakeholders.

Finally, expressing gratitude and celebrating small victories can provide motivation and encouragement. 1 Thessalonians 5:18 (NIV) advises, "Give thanks in all circumstances; for this is God's will for you in Christ Jesus." Acknowledging progress and expressing gratitude for God's blessings, even amidst challenges, fosters a positive outlook and strengthens faith.

In conclusion, navigating challenges with faith involves seeking God's guidance through prayer, embracing a positive mindset, relying on scripture, seeking support from a community of believers, developing resilience, maintaining integrity, and expressing gratitude. By integrating these strategies, businesses can face challenges with confidence, resilience, and trust in God's plan. As you navigate obstacles, remember the wisdom of Joshua 1:9 (NIV): "Have I not commanded you? Be strong and courageous. Do not be afraid; do not be discouraged, for the Lord your God will be with you wherever you go." Let this principle guide your journey, ensuring that your business honors God and reflects His glory.

Chapter 15

Legacy and Impact

Leaving a Lasting Mark

The ultimate goal of a faith-based business is to leave a lasting legacy that honors God and positively impacts the community and future generations. Proverbs 13:22 (NIV) states, "A good person leaves an inheritance for their children's children, but a sinner's wealth is stored up for the righteous." This chapter explores how to create a legacy that reflects biblical values, ensuring that the business's impact endures.

The foundation of a lasting legacy is a clear and compelling vision. Proverbs 29:18 (NIV) emphasizes, "Where there is no vision, the people perish." Defining a long-term vision that aligns with biblical principles and encompasses the business's mission, values, and goals provides direction and purpose. This vision serves as a guiding star, ensuring that all actions and decisions contribute to a meaningful legacy.

Mentorship and succession planning are critical for sustaining the business's values and mission. 2 Timothy 2:2 (NIV) advises, "And the things you have heard me say in the presence of many witnesses entrust to reliable people who will also be qualified to teach others." Identifying and mentoring future leaders who share the business's values ensures continuity and preserves the business's faith-driven culture. This intentional investment in the next generation fosters a legacy of integrity and service.

Philanthropy and community involvement are essential components of a lasting impact. Acts 20:35 (NIV) reminds us, "In everything I did, I showed you that by this kind of hard work we must help the weak, remembering the words the Lord Jesus himself said: 'It is more blessed to give than to receive.'" Supporting charitable causes, engaging in community service, and promoting social justice reflect the business's commitment to serving God's kingdom. These actions create a positive and lasting impact on the community and beyond.

Environmental stewardship contributes to a sustainable legacy. Genesis 2:15 (NIV) highlights our responsibility to care for creation: "The Lord God took the man and put him in the Garden of Eden to work it and take care of it." Implementing sustainable practices, reducing environmental impact, and advocating for conservation efforts ensure that the business leaves a positive legacy for future generations. This commitment to stewardship honors God and protects His creation.

Documenting the business's history, values, and achievements can inspire future generations and preserve the business's legacy. Deuteronomy 6:6-7 (NIV) advises, "These commandments that I give you today are to be on your hearts. Impress them on your children. Talk about them when you sit at home and when you walk along the road, when you lie down and when you get up." Creating written records, such as a company history, values statement, and testimonials, ensures that the business's story and principles are passed down.

Encouraging a culture of continuous improvement and innovation ensures that the business remains relevant and impactful. Isaiah 43:19 (NIV) says, "See, I am doing a new thing! Now it springs up; do you not perceive it?" Embracing change, seeking new opportunities, and encouraging creativity within the organization fosters growth and adaptability. This forward-thinking mindset ensures that the business can navigate future challenges and continue making a positive impact.

In conclusion, creating a lasting legacy involves defining a clear vision, mentorship and succession planning, philanthropy and community involvement, environmental stewardship, documenting the business's history, and fostering continuous improvement and innovation. By integrating these elements, businesses can leave a legacy that honors God and positively impacts future generations. As you strive to create a lasting legacy, remember the wisdom of Matthew 5:16 (NIV): "In the same way, let your light shine before others, that they may see your good deeds and glorify your Father in heaven." Let this principle guide your efforts, ensuring that your business reflects your faith and serves God's kingdom for generations to come.

Leaving a lasting legacy also involves nurturing relationships and fostering a sense of community within and outside the business. Hebrews 10:24-25 (NIV) encourages, "And let us consider how we may spur one another on toward love and good deeds, not giving up meeting together, as some are in the habit of doing, but encouraging one another." Building strong relationships with employees, clients, and partners creates a network of support and shared values that endures beyond the immediate business operations.

Celebrating milestones and recognizing contributions is essential for reinforcing the business's values and achievements. Psalm 145:4 (NIV) states, "One generation commends your works to another; they tell of your mighty acts." Regularly acknowledging the hard work and dedication of employees, as well as celebrating business achievements, fosters a sense of pride and continuity.

This recognition helps ensure that the business's legacy of excellence and service is remembered and appreciated.

Additionally, fostering a culture of ethical decision-making and integrity ensures that the business's legacy is built on a solid foundation. Proverbs 20:7 (NIV) highlights the importance of integrity: "The righteous lead blameless lives; blessed are their children after them." By maintaining high ethical standards and prioritizing honesty and transparency, businesses can build a reputation that stands the test of time. This ethical legacy attracts loyal customers and employees who value integrity and trust.

Implementing educational programs and initiatives that align with the business's mission can also extend its impact. Providing scholarships, sponsoring educational events, and supporting learning opportunities for employees and the community reflects a commitment to personal and professional growth. Proverbs 1:5 (NIV) advises, "Let the wise listen and add to their learning, and let the discerning get guidance." Investing in education fosters a knowledgeable and empowered community that carries forward the business's values.

Finally, embracing technology and innovation can ensure that the business remains relevant and impactful in a rapidly changing world. Ecclesiastes 3:1 (NIV) reminds us, "There is a time for everything, and a season for every activity under the heavens." Staying abreast of technological advancements and integrating innovative solutions into business operations demonstrates adaptability and forward-thinking. This proactive approach ensures that the business can continue to thrive and make a positive impact in the future.

In conclusion, leaving a lasting legacy involves nurturing relationships, celebrating achievements, fostering ethical decision-making, implementing educational programs, and embracing innovation. By integrating these elements, businesses can create a legacy that honors God and positively impacts future generations. As you strive to leave a lasting mark, remember the wisdom of Psalm 78:4 (NIV): "We will not hide them from their descendants; we will tell the next generation the praiseworthy deeds of the Lord, his power, and the wonders he has done." Let this principle guide your efforts, ensuring that your business reflects your faith and serves God's kingdom for generations to come.

By committing to these principles and integrating them into every aspect of your business, you not only ensure the success and sustainability of your enterprise but also create a powerful testimony of faith in action. Your business becomes a beacon of hope, integrity, and service in the community, shining a light that inspires others to follow. In the end, the true measure of success is not just in the profits earned or the milestones achieved, but in the lasting impact made and the lives touched by your unwavering commitment to God's principles.

Epilogue

Reflecting on the Journey

84

As we come to the end of this exploration of integrating biblical principles into business, it is important to reflect on the journey and the lessons learned. Building a business that honors God, serves the community, and leaves a lasting legacy is a noble and rewarding endeavor. It is a journey that requires faith, dedication, and a commitment to living out one's values in every aspect of business operations.

Throughout this book, we have delved into the many facets of operating a faith-based business. From establishing a strong foundation of ethical practices and servant leadership to balancing profit and purpose, each chapter has provided insights and practical strategies for integrating faith into business. By anchoring your business in biblical principles, you create an environment where integrity, trust, and service thrive.

One of the key takeaways from this journey is the importance of aligning your business's mission with God's purpose. Proverbs 16:3 (NIV) reminds us, "Commit to the Lord whatever you do, and he will establish your plans." When your business is rooted in a higher purpose, it not only achieves financial success but also contributes to the greater good. This alignment brings a sense of fulfillment and peace, knowing that your work is part of God's plan.

Another crucial lesson is the value of building and nurturing relationships. Business is fundamentally about people—employees, clients, partners, and the community. By fostering a culture of trust, respect, and empathy, you create a supportive and collaborative environment that benefits everyone involved. Hebrews 10:24 (NIV) encourages us, "And let us consider how we may spur one another on toward love and good deeds." Strong relationships are the bedrock of a successful and impactful business.

The journey of integrating faith into business is also about resilience and adaptability. Challenges and obstacles are inevitable, but with faith and perseverance, they can be overcome. James 1:2-4 (NIV) teaches us, "Consider it pure joy, my brothers and sisters, whenever you face trials of many kinds, because you know that the testing of your faith produces perseverance. Let perseverance finish its work so that you may be mature and complete, not lacking anything." Embracing challenges as opportunities for growth strengthens your resolve and enhances your ability to navigate the complexities of business.

Generosity and stewardship are integral to a faith-based business. By managing resources wisely and giving back to the community, you reflect God's love and grace. Acts 20:35 (NIV) reminds us, "It is more blessed to give than to receive." Generosity not only enriches the lives of others but also brings joy and fulfillment to the giver. It creates a ripple effect of positivity that extends far beyond the immediate business context.

As you reflect on the principles and strategies discussed in this book, remember that the journey of faith in business is ongoing. It requires continuous learning, growth, and a steadfast commitment to living out your values. Surround yourself with a community of believers who can provide support, encouragement, and accountability. Seek God's guidance in all your decisions, trusting that He will lead you on the right path.

In conclusion, operating a business based on biblical principles is a powerful way to honor God and make a positive impact in the world. It is a journey that transforms not only your business but also your life and the lives of those around you. As you continue on this path, may you find strength, wisdom, and joy in knowing that you are fulfilling God's purpose for your life and your business.

Remember the words of Jeremiah 29:11 (NIV): "For I know the plans I have for you," declares the Lord, "plans to prosper you and not to harm you, plans to give you hope and a future." Trust in His plans, and let your business be a testament to His love, grace, and faithfulness.

Thank you for embarking on this journey with me. May God bless you and your business abundantly as you strive to honor Him in all that you do.

Don't miss out!

Visit the website below and you can sign up to receive emails whenever Diana Gadus, M.Ed. publishes a new book. There's no charge and no obligation.

https://books2read.com/r/B-A-UNSUB-SHIDE

BOOKS 2 READ

Connecting independent readers to independent writers.

About the Author

Diana Gadus, M.Ed., is a distinguished real estate professional and seasoned educator with over two decades of experience. Holding two Master's degrees in Education, specializing in School Counseling and Educational Leadership, Diana brings a unique blend of expertise to her career. She has earned prestigious designations including Committed to Excellence, Senior Real Estate Specialist, and Resort and Second Home Property Specialist. As the founder of Savvy Florida Agent, Diana is renowned for her unwavering commitment to ethical business practices, community service, and integrating faith into her professional endeavors. Her extensive background in education and real estate, coupled with her faith-driven approach, uniquely qualifies her to guide others in building businesses that honor God and positively impact their communities. Above all, Diana's greatest achievements and joys are birthing and raising her six children, who inspire her daily commitment to excellence and integrity.

Read more at https://www.dianagadus.com.

About the Publisher

Diana Gadus, M.Ed., is a distinguished real estate professional, seasoned educator, and accomplished author. With over two decades of experience in education, holding two Master's degrees in Education specializing in School Counseling and Educational Leadership, Diana has seamlessly integrated her extensive expertise into her writing and publishing endeavors. She has earned notable designations such as Committed to Excellence, Senior Real Estate Specialist, and Resort and Second Home Property Specialist, reflecting her dedication to professionalism and ethical practices.

As the founder and publisher of her own publishing business, Diana Gadus, M.Ed., is committed to producing works that inspire, educate, and empower. Her publishing company focuses on creating content that integrates biblical principles with practical strategies, offering readers valuable insights into faith-based living and ethical business practices. Diana's passion for helping others succeed is evident in every book she publishes, ensuring that each work is a testament to integrity, trust, and service. With a deep commitment to her faith and community, Diana's publishing business is dedicated to making a positive and lasting impact on readers worldwide.

Read more at https://dianagadus.com.

9 798227 528766